ʒt praise for judith vollmer:

The Water Books (Autumn House Press, 2012)

"Above all, [Vollmer] has an unerring ability to arrive at those moments when quotidian objects and events are suddenly given the aura of something more vast and more vexing: call it historical force."

—David Wojahn

"*The Water Books* is a remarkable achievement for its tough wit and shimmering beauties. Vollmer's Rome and Pittsburgh meet as vivid—equally adored—parallel gem-lines in a magnanimous space. These poems are feats of a heightened, familial, and adhesive consciousness, very good news for us all."

—Anne Waldman

Reactor (University of Wisconsin Press, 2004)

"If Literature is 'a study in comparative humanity,' and I think it is, *Reactor* places new emphasis on our complicitous age of nuclear fission at all levels of conscientiousness, in the strategies of highbrow expatriates, and Vollmer's identification with the 'lowest of the low' wayfaring strangers, a high-wire act among her pantheon of peasant witnesses. We have a new vocabulary of songmaking, ancient and modern."

—Michael S. Harper

"In *Reactor*, Vollmer explores the exercise of power—familial, literary, nuclear, political. The contaminating 'silver coin of plutonium' races through these poems, casting an eerie glow. Read *Reactor* and let Vollmer refresh your geography in startling ways."

—Robin Becker

The Door Open to the Fire (Cleveland State University Press, 1997)

"The subject—the obsession—of this book is place; the particular focus of both its rage and its love is the American city. What is amazing is the book's exemplary originality."

—Lynn Emanuel

"Vollmer's embrace is so wide, her enthusiasm for participation in the streaming variations of life so evident, that these poems sweep us up in their energies, their flesh-and-blood longings, their deeply human sense of helplessness and hope. This is a citizen's testament, as passionate and complicated as a great city demands."

—Mark Doty

Level Green (University of Wisconsin Press, 1990)

"Judith Vollmer writes with sweet agility and moving force. Her poems have an electric energy, and they have compassion, as they stand witness to personal happiness, inquiry, anger—as they bear the knowledge of the political and spiritual cripplings of our time."

—Mary Oliver

"In poem after poem, Vollmer's *Level Green* reveals the pains and glories of America's raging urban reality. Radically real—generous, social, sensual, smart—*Level Green* is loaded with humanity, solidarity, and love."

—Lawrence Joseph

THE
apoLLonia poems

WISCONSIN POETRY SERIES

Ronald Wallace, *Series Editor*

the
apolLonia
poems

Judith Vollmer

THE UNIVERSITY OF WISCONSIN PRESS

Publication of this volume has been made possible, in part, through support from the Brittingham Fund.

The University of Wisconsin Press
1930 Monroe Street, 3rd Floor
Madison, Wisconsin 53711-2059
uwpress.wisc.edu

3 Henrietta Street, Covent Garden
London WC2E 8LU, United Kingdom
eurospanbookstore.com

Printed in the United States of America

This book may be available in a digital edition.

LIBRARY OF CONGRESS CATALOGING-IN-PUBLICATION DATA

Names: Vollmer, Judith, 1951– author.
Title: The Apollonia poems / Judith Vollmer.
Other titles: Wisconsin poetry series.
Description: Madison, Wisconsin: The University of Wisconsin Press, [2017] |
    Series: Wisconsin poetry series
Identifiers: LCCN 2016041568 | ISBN 9780299312848 (pbk.: alk. paper)
Subjects: | LCGFT: Poetry.
Classification: LCC PS3572.O3957 A86 2017 | DDC 811/.54—dc23 LC
    record available at https://lccn.loc.gov/2016041568

for Ann

and for

Peter Oresick
1955–2016
druzhba

Apollonia:—ancient cities in Albania, Bulgaria, Greece, Sicily

—3rd Century A.D. woman claimed as martyr and saint

—deity of light called The Destroyer

contents

I.

II.   the apollonia sequence

acknowledgments

Thanks are due to the editors of the journals in which the following poems—some under different titles or in different forms—have appeared:

    Connotation Press: "Children of October"
    Great River Review: "I Don't Want to Wake Her," "Street Grate," "After Reading Another Book of Dull Poetry, I Go Out and Cut the Grass," and "The Transfer"
    Miramar: "The Great Lakes" and "12th Ward"
    Pittsburgh Poetry Review: "Flower Meal" and "My Mother's Paintings"
    Poetry International: "Little Death"
    Prairie Schooner: "In an Old Hotel" in the "Women and the Global Imagination" issue edited by Alicia Ostriker
    The Stillwater Review: "Last Effects, Old House" and "Another Green"
    Women Write Resistance: Poets Resist Gender Violence, edited by Laura Madeline Wiseman: "The Shape-up"

I would also like to thank the Corporation of Yaddo and the American Academy in Rome for residencies that provided me with solitude in which to work; the University of Pittsburgh at Greensburg for travel support; and the writing community in the Drew University MFA Program in Poetry & Poetry in Translation. Deep appreciation goes to the staff at the University of Wisconsin Press, with particular thanks to Wisconsin Poetry Series editor Ron Wallace for his support of my work over the years. And I send my heartfelt gratitude to Stephen Dau, Stephanie Flom, Timothy Gebadlo, Geeta Kothari, Ted Lardner, Anne Marie Macari, Shannon Sankey, Mary Taylor Simeti, Eva Simms, Erjola Tafaj, Maureen M. Squires, Marian Vollmer, and Michael Wurster; and, most of all, to Jan Beatty, Ed Ochester, Gerald Stern, and Michael Waters.

I.

Stranger: Whom were you waiting for?

Endymion: We musn't speak her name. Don't speak her name.
She has no name—or she has many.

—Cesare Pavese

Another Green

—closing the old house

Everything got more complicated after I wrote
the 4 notes on scrap paper, tucked them

NorthEastSouthWest and Skip came with his pickup & icepack
of Yuenglings to help me load last things, and the sad woman pulled into the drive

would I buy a party door   a giant automated mesh garage door perfect
in summer especially like now, buggy, & rain falling all this last

night   The notes I hid
hum inside the walls and I want them quiet

watching over like eyes on the street   out here where there is no street
only ex-urban speedway   once a lane of mailboxes

emptied one afternoon by a small girl   she's learning to read, opens the aluminum
doors   lowers the red flags & sorts her white dove-pets under the forsythia

reverie until mother, mailman & neighbors arrive   She says
I'm working   but really it's a party under the wide screen

of the bush   trying to read messages of strangers without
leaving the bower's fresh green she loves more than anything.

Window with Bottles

Dusk presses in through the screen
thick, riffed by breeze.
The bottles turn & swivel on their sill, changing

places. Cherry brandy, blue apothecary,
Scotch decanter from *Our Mutual Friend*,
green Trebbiano tilts its neck toward a cove.

They are listening for vibrations that might make
a bottle song: low notes to high, fat bass,
smoky mezzo, a high-res flute silvering the screen

faster than the speed of sound
down to the marshes, further to the groves
where wind hissing inside reeds

first taught men of the country
to blow through hollow stalks.
They learned their sweet songs

along pathless woods & glades, among the deserted
places of the shepherds, and during their only leisure.
This soothed their minds and delighted them
along with fullness of food,
for then everything is congenial.

While the bottles sing   I want to
breathe out & catch on an ease
to relieve her sadness.

Walking to *Miami*

—*Gelateria Miami, Piazza Francesco Cucchi 8, Rome*

1

Finish Cernuda notes   shut computer   Hydrate, grab
envelope   Ciao, Luca   avoid Louisa at curb   long stroll on twilit
Marmorata   Cross Tiber at Sublico   quick turn   drop envelope
in Eugenia's slot   Yesterday Besa told me:
>   "I wanted to buy a computer? Government paperwork. Interview.
>   No go." (Albanian passport & deadlined temp visa only) She's here
>   10 years, brilliant student & steady at work

Graffiti tags unspool righteously against 28%
no/jobs/for/youth/here   like home, where our
percentages, though less, get cooked

"Distance teaches," Will Self wrote after walking to New York
from London (well, there was the plane), but he trekked the M25
Stockwell to Heathrow, flew across the pond
& walked Kennedy to Ground Zero
wedged against the guardrails
>   You walked *where?*
>   everyone asks my friend Patrick who walks Brooklyn
>   to the Y, & Camden to Drew   "It takes time, so you have to
>   map it & forget being a social sentient being."

        Turn, stop a sec, hydrate   hamstrings micro-adjust
toward the 74 steps crenellated & complete
as if released from deep inside the Janiculum
fully formed   sudden Mobius lifting me up
into the first stirrings of night air
Men cut, carved, carried this stone
marking perfect depth of field for feet of the thirsty
climbing up to the great aqueduct   Seven sources channeled
from the countryside down & into three vast tanks

2

From Minerva's ruined temple-marble rose Il Fontanone
        I don't "divide my time" between x & y
        Time splits me   I head up   feel the heaviness
        Then I lighten, summit & stroll, & slow
        Under the bluing sky before the pool
        & falls, five bays tumbling like burst spigots
        spewing escalators
        downward cooling the city

My mouth waters for the vanished
summer garden behind the iron grille,
to sit under jasmine with a silver bowl & spoon: *Cosa vorresti?*
        Some of each, my brothers would say,
        all eyes on Dad opening the Sealtest
        half-gallon & pausing to display the American/
        Neapolitan block, the long knife, & the carving:
        for each plate, equal slab: chocolate, vanilla,
        strawberry, cross-wise   I half-circle behind the great
        fountain, street still slanting upward

3

Cross Carini—West   turn right down Francesco Daverio
He died defending the hill for the Republic
           and arrive under the pink & green neon tubes
           among starched pensioners & kids in Vans
           queuing in the doorway beneath the dayglo

        Art Deco scroll:::::*Miami*:::::

I never get why my Italian friends
fly to New York & turn left fast
for the other South
when everything here is touched by the sea

Perfume of mango   almond   tangerine   darkest chocolate *con panna*
per favore   mouth waters   & apricot because now is the season
& Italy produces the most in the EU-28

4

Tiny port   far from Lesbos, Lampedusa, Calais, souls washing ashore
flung onto stones in hopes of safety   Our faces

reflected in the 4th World Cup 2006 posters,
faces framed & glassy, riding the surf of the hot pink wall   We inch closer

> wedges of lime   lemon wheels
> bundletts of cherries in a clay bowl beside Benedetta

> taking our orders in black stilettos & pressed black pencil skirt
> immaculate lace at her clavicle framing a small silver cross

Madonna   it says, and   *Mare*

Madonna of the Sea,
  Are you lost?   Are you waiting for someone?

Benedetta rings the register
guarded by Neptune

whose marble eyes emit a bright white

Children of October

Those of us born in July, voluptuous & moody,
frost the sun with our loneliness.

Under hottest skies we sing to the hidden moon.
Those born in July are children of October

carrying bushels of peaches
home, never too early to stock up, take

home wherever we go, buoyant as saltwater
showing off
our rare equilibrium
conceived in October

when two fall to the floor, laughing
in search of a lost earring.
Those of us born in July

carry our opposite season
as the willow does, she lets

long green hair down, turning flexible head
down to brush the weeds & clasp

tufts of rabbit fur into
her slender olivine leaves
dressing for the cold, always
last to drop leaves,
first to show her bitter-soft mud-yellow tongues.

The Great Lakes

Suckle the great blue swollen
lungs, many-breasted, multi-
graped clusters, now I know
joy is impersonal,
swelling makes me full, pausing
like a sleepy baby gorging
passing out from it. Gaze into
blue so viscous
though it has been oil-
streaked, set fire to,
dredged for ore,
shat into by the great ships
of Commodore Perry,
pissed into by me encouraged to do so
by my Baci who said in Polish
my mother translating,
"It is vast & clean & takes away
all the germs from winter long."
Joy impersonal
eyeball to infant cells
inside Erie's
stopped-down gray cape of clouds
& heron, ceiling of feathers,
water over my 4-year-old head
unspeeding above me
it seems eternal though I have
no such language then.

White Box   Blue Lid

Suppose an insane wind holds all the hills

In the event of an active shooter
one JAMBLOCK for each classroom
will I   whose wounds
1 bottle hydrogen peroxide   1 flash light   2 extra batteries
Block door w/ bar   what will I   save them

sturdy for common things

1 roll toilet paper   1 roll 10 trash bags   1 roll paper towel
3 pairs latex gloves 10bandaids30cottonballs1bottlehandsanitizer
on the training video, bar in locked position
Will I be   how to defend   wounds

cling to the earth

Save myself   Who will inherit   Who
knows the voice of the real police?
See someone coming
In the event of an active shooter   how to get out
through the safety-sealed windows
what will I   lockdown

love where we are

voices of students
White box blue lid   do not open   except in the event
1 roll duct tape   1 ace bandage
Stevie's hand under the chair   Rachel's chipped teeth
NO HUNTINGALCOHOLFIREARMS the campus entrance commands
Today we

locate ourselves by the real things

Today I'll scan for them
William Stafford's masterpiece *"Allegiances"*

I Don't Want to Wake Her

I never trusted you, never

knew if you'd be where you said you were.
Too late my fault   I swerve her chair

into the salon   lift her to the wall of mirrors
select her pencil, pancake, coral
lips. Her hairspray clots

her re-wind: *I never knew where*
you were, if you'd come, but

she's relaxed, awake now and I feel
the light panic, how long to the bell.
If you'd been a boy I'd

just have thought, 'Oh, he's here
& there' and I wouldn't have cared.

The sweet dollop of her laugh
opens the lane
past carts & vials & bright

doors leaking after-dinner stench & scented
wreaths for every season back to the cube she calls

My House. Are you happy? We reversed time
when we made this replica house:

staged it with the blue painting & old
dresser's song of sliding drawers—

Am I happy when she is, in the open window & sole
pine tree's turpentine scent. Soon she will

      pound on the door
      of her old house till the new
      owners let us in, a dead woman &

      her girl circling until they find the window
      facing Sulfur Creek, restored
      & stocked with perch
      in their absence, stretching itself
      along the tall marsh grasses.

Two Women

Betsy never thought my annual solo
Dickens fest nor my adulteries odd. Nor
my little black book of 197_ recording our
male pressroom colleagues, as in, "ELEVATOR
SCENE: in which A.E. hisses to his 4
cronies as our best-girl reporter friend steps on:
'Whose cunt smells?' Big laughs as she steps off."
Behind the modesty panels of our female desks
or in the female smoking lounge (men lit up
at their desks), we plotted. She trained, taught,
covered for me as we worked The Rim
editing, calculating headlines, and when we were
promoted to clearing Page 1 in the composing room:
no typos in the 96-point heads, or your job:
first question from the guys on our return,
"Did you get it in?" B danced, read Russian
in Pittsburgh & St. Petersburg, reviewed
bestsellers & unknowns. I wrote poems on breaks
& went to grad school. We cooked, drank,
worked on no sleep, wrote, wrote, mostly
read: Brookner, Gallant, Austen, the young
Alice Walker, Trollope, Forster, Durrell, Hurston,
Lessing; all the men all the women, the famous
& modest, & Drabble who seemed to know us.
Over drinks, after nightshift, B said, "Why don't
you write to her, ask for an interview? She's probably
a delight, it'll be fun." I reread everything, made
my questions, then wrote, and when her reply came
I went to London. Afternoon on Russell Square
over the tiny Sony. More next day over coffee
& Scotch. Home, the 6 cassettes garbled,
transcript attempted, interview drafted. Way
too long, an editor, then 2 more, said, & another.
I shelved it during a love crisis; dejected, wrote
my embarrassed apology, promptly
lost the manuscript for 14 years.

"I'm such a stupid girl," I cried, 197_, then we laughed
how I wore sunglasses the first time I bought condoms.
I liked women I liked men, I wore my diaphragm
all the time thinking I could be spontaneous.
B listened deep, talked me down, we'd plan
our next party. We marched, wrote, wrote, fought
for women editors, lunches for kids, houses with
windows instead of boards, girls in sports, boys
in the kitchen. We were mad all the time   yeah
and wrote & told everybody so.
B & I thought Drabble our favorite writer
might be the kind of person who seems to have
the capacity for living alone & thinking
about things & asking difficult questions
about history, while most of us live lives
of days interrupted and that we are utterly
fragmented & scattered around.

B quit The Rim and moved
west: real critic job. *Kansas City Star*
& thousands of stories improved by her eye & hand.
I taught, wandered, listening for poems.
Both of us married. Calls & postcards. I abandoned
people, fell asleep, woke up very slowly

then woke in a panic reading her column: B recounting
her diagnosis & epic surgery. I picked up
the phone, we resumed after 15 years.
She moved back to town.
We cooked for each other & mutual friends.
B & Bill taped *The West Wing* for me
nights I had to teach. B'd taught a generation
of apprentice critics how to write about books,
dance, food in the manner of MFK Fisher.
I finally understood Drabble's enormous & public
erudition rose from her mother/daughter/sib/wife
gossipy-caustic Londoner web of wit. I was trying

to finish a book and that winter
B read it for sound, bullshit, sense. " . . . this one
gives us a rationing of details that has
a riveting effect, a sense of being sucked under
against our will. It's lovely & dark, so stay
dark, keep going," she said,

about something I'd nearly dropped.
"Simplify. Stop diverting yourself from the obsessions."
She knew I was working through the nights
and every Saturday morning she'd
drop a brioche or muffin with a video or new
book in my door on her way home from weekly
marketing, rain or shine, chemo or no.

I became her sous-chef our last winter.
We went to the opera, met in the coffeehouses,
she baked till she filled everybody's freezers, then
taught me how to make 4 kinds of sorbet.
We planted tomatoes & peppers, transplanted
tarragon, and sat on her porch talking without stopping.
I found the lost Drabble interview
while unpacking old boxes after a move. We walked
Trillium Trail, & the uphill path to the old
bocce courts, then wandered the park back
to her porch in the early spring afternoons. My
Fortune, my Persephone, Betsy, my Elizabeth.

In an Old Hotel

In for the night I empty my pockets,
gallery stub, train card, what's left of all my 20s,
and the crushed bloom—Who placed it
in my hand, was she a new immigrant, or
a hedgefund girl who walked into my 23rd Street
daydream & said "Eat the body of this flower"—
What is this spiky beauty, a tiny sister
to the giant pine cone pillaged for the Vatican
that Dante snarled into an enemy's prickly face?
Cone scepter in the hand of an Egyptian queen?
Maybe it's arrived
from home & the carnival of daisy-stars in our yard—
fleabane or aster or the great purplehead itself,
echinacea spinning its seed stories of the Lenape
healers who practiced its three dozen uses.
Tincture w/ goldenseal is my cold cure.
The little cone funnels me into solitude in this old hotel,
eating hours, chewing them to delicious powder,
into good work—like good hash, made by hand,
sieves, scissors. Emperor Shen Nung doled out hash
for beriberi, "female weakness," malaria, & absent
mindedness in 2737 B.C. My sore eyes &
crooked Baci fingers ease while I smoke
& sweeten my enemies, myself, in my room's
unfinished wall repair, a fresco-
field I dream on while adjusting the brass
screen to my pipe, pleasure in
handling this gift of kief, carving it into dusky
blonde curls. Strike the match again and enter
another country suffused with smoky texture
of my love's kiss sending me off through the gate.

The Transfer

When a night courier brakes at my curb
I lay eyes on it for the first time
large & broad, spot-lit under the streetlamp
      wrapped in batting
      braced between birch boards

I run down to the street
and the driver & I lift   glide it off
like a slippery page from a far seafloor

and en route back up my walk
I notice the sky
shift to first-light
and when we reach my door I see
my neighbor leaning
washing her open casement window

that mirrors the unseen held in our arms

I catch in her glass a full second
—a shroud, anointed but not human—

     the canvas
passing swiftly into my house

now unwrapped & lifted onto
the one wall big enough to hold it
while the half-light the courier disappears back into
brightens, so I drowse & brew coffee

     less than 20 feet from the panel shimmering
     peach & goldfoil, warming my November house
     & lighting it with tapers of cream-bits &

making the rooms seem much smaller
      against the panel's many seas & inlets whose
clotted marine-teal cell clusters
      shoot cobalt wands through my tiny archways
         & vestibule until the wall itself begins a crackling sound;

Icy runnels bubble the plaster,
baseboards & seams extend & split
& open so my complete north
         wall lifts itself

up & back a foot,
six more in a hyperdraft lift-away.

What I once thought about paint
was soft & dangerous

until my house burst
until I was visited by the fire world
      of Joan Mitchell.
      I find myself

looking over the side-yard's
line of hemlocks, the panel
      attaching fronds to itself
speeding backward
while I breathe first fresh air of winter.

12th Ward

My table at the old New Meadow
Grill on Larimer Avenue has a window
on Ferlo's new farm—kids picking lettuce
for the first time and I'm translating
poems stamped onto the white tin ceiling my
uncle nailed to the lathe; I curse
the catpiss wine for 3 seconds, but I'm half a city away
from the streets where flower wreaths hang
from custom-made iron spikes. I'm eating and
going to eat while the kids unpave the broken
curbs so wild cresses can grow, and they're
lining a wheelbarrow with behemoth spring
greens Mrs. Lemon will chop into the sweet
onion layers of the 12th Ward. I'm long-gone
from the forced narcissi people
opening their mouths to white caviar & shouting
about themselves on F***book. I was thrilled
when they laid me on ice and ecstatic
when they tossed me onto the back of the open truck.

The Vowel

—Etruscan sarcophagus, Villa Giulia, Rome

I stared at her braids   afraid she was
Universal   and I was locked

    onto the earth-vowel she seemed to be mouthing
reclining at her wedding feast, hands full of grapes

    bronze bracelets aglow
                Did her mouth flute a warning

    moaning up
        through the long braids
    threading the roof of her mouth
        to the top of her head
             coiling down, nape stretching into a thicket
out there—outside the walls—?

The braids
    threaded a map   divided my head into many parts
    starched white in French braids
    my mother plaited each morning
    till my eyes watered,
    I wound myself
around books

until, above half-
moon earlobes, a voice:
    You were conceived three times before you were born.

I was   bull-headed
and bore stone-
sounds that could
carry me anywhere.

Woman on the tomb,
                              Destroyer,
to what myth
                    did I first lose myself?

Apollonia Is Restored to the Book

We already know
why Anonymous did not step forward
to speak
to sign her canvas:

(adultery   rape & shame   abortion
burials   slanders of forgery, parody, plagiarism;
worst: shyness of her own genius)

but my Apollonia
was bound to a young Polish soldier
from the Vistula, sent to Italy, War of 1866.

Her birth name carried from Pollina,
north, east via Bari, & Turkey, east
to the green-cold Carpathians.

Who removed her name
from the ledger of the old church?
Who penciled it back in?

II.

the apollonia sequence

I've buried childhood at the bottom of my nights
and now it divides me
from everything like an invisible blade.

—Giuseppe Ungaretti

Voices in this sequence are, in order of appearance:

Mała Babka
Granddaughter
Mother

Mała Babka Pays an Evening Visit, Rolls Down Her Stockings and Looks Around

You want to fix something in this world? Clean your own house first.

Me? What's that bag of shoes you carry around?
If you're not wearing them, throw them out.

Can't wear shoes of the dead. You have to bury them. I want coffee.

Let me get you a shovel.

You want to make things neat in your head. Me, I read the papers.

Ha—*Jaskółka*: 1915 edition, Rzeszów's finest weekly.

Fires, money sickness, fighting there too. Here it's better. Was worst down in Shtinkin Halloh.

Sticker Hollow—named for the thorn-bushes & hawthorns along the river!
Didn't we call them jaggerbushes? Did we eat hawthorn berries?

In tea. And I found you gooseberries. I made you rose-hip for your colds.

And you put honey in it. Did we eat meat-cakes?

Payday, when the bosses handed out scrip
He came all the way across the ocean
One man among many
The Poles   the Rusyns—all the Slavs the same
Who else could take 120 degrees & lift beams & crawl down holes?
Slaves—I say the word!
One among many   he ran from war   ran from the copper mines
        so he could climb down inside Frick's shtinkin holes!

Did you wrap his feet in newspapers in winter? Did we eat sour cream & rye bread?

Sour cream I made myself   bread I made   onions & garlic I snipped for the top
Of course I wrapped his feet

Then I went down and played with the baskets.

I let you go down to the little cellar because you were good.
This coffee is good! like mine   like tar   give me some chocolate
I let you go down to the golden onions
        to teach you tears can be sweet

Did we burn coal and breathe it day & night?
Did our rags turn black?

I have rags of every color—[laughs]
Ivory from bleaching   red & brown from bleedings
Green from garden   black from coughing

In the holloh house I looked down through cracks
        in the boards and saw yellow water running from the mines
When rains came
        yellow water could wash us all away—

Before the Face of Matki Bożej Czestochowa

Before the face of Matki Bożej Czestochowa
  our parents set our match America was set
He came alone on a ship
I came alone on a ship six months after
  with Janina, age two years, my neighbor's child

No, Mała Babka. No match. He took you
from the town of Pollina, née Apollonia.
A lonely Polish soldier fighting for Prussia in Italy.
He bought you took you
through Bari, through Turkey, & back to Poland.

You're confusing me with my own Mała Babka—
You think you're smart?
Long before you were two years
  you could talk in sentences
   but did not stand or walk
I sent you down the stone steps—your own mother crying—to the cellar

To shut me up—my mother couldn't.
I sang on our top kitchen step but couldn't
stand or walk. My mother propped me against a chair when we went visiting.

Your mother thought she would live forever
That is why she was so long in her house
  and why you had to take her away from it
  and move her into the place.

She hated the place when she talked to us.
Loved the place when she held court.
Queen of her meal table!

This was her bittersweetness & suffering

You weren't there! Or were you
passing back & forth through the veils?

Very Smart   Very Proud

Yet your mother suffered over the quickness of life
You
Sad sometimes
like me,
you think you know things?

I know women will be last.
My eyes ache.

You have too many books.

I have my house, my love. Books enough for a while—

You know things?

I know a lot of things. I know
they rape & sell girls. I know
they want to close a girls' school? Easy:
throw poison down a well.
Women, children, animals. All will be last.

Women. [Spits.]
Women cry & bleat & manipulate
I have done these things myself
            so I know!

If a woman breaks your heart, it's broken twice,
and you yourself a woman
helped it along. I've done this myself.
But
they use us. They write laws   threats   laws on our bodies   we
let them use us.
In Poland you left school before it was time, and your teacher cried.

Shut!!! I learned to read first!
Let me tell you girls & boys & old & young
All suffered
And more suffer now

Old Polish Songs

And you taught me old Polish songs.

[They sing together:]

It's so wonderful to have another little war
so we can have a parade.
See—the soldier rides his horse into the village
so he can be seen by the girl
who's pretty as a painted picture—

When he falls from his horse
they play a beautiful song for his bravery!

I hate that song.

You hate the truth.

You were always whispering & rasping into your rosary.

I'll teach you a prayer I made for your uncle in 1934:

Little brother
Walk across the smallest iron bridge
Two miles downriver
You'll see my yellow porch & stack of wood
My door's unlocked
Leave tonight!

He was taken out of school and put to work.
Age 13 years, put to work on Troy Hill, put to sleep in a truck farm bunk.

Once you're poor you stay that way
But it is America
It is August and today I found
            so many pears! All along the walk—
No one in that big house
            even knew they had a tree

Will you make me a song?

        [Mała Babka sings:]

        You cry, you cry when you're happy, like me
        Cried when you said your first words:
        Crawl   Up   Kitchen   Steps
        You held a crayon in your fist
        And drew a long strand of grass
        Onto the lip of the top step!

She Pours Wisniak into Their Coffee Cups

Drink to
nectar of the sour cherry tree   talking in our ways   holding up four corners
         of the house
Coffee!   Night!   singing in our ways!

Sun came this morning   wasn't that a surprise
Always so much clouds in this godforsaken river town

I fell hard while still a girl
         so the match was a gift   The old ones saw our eyes

My soldier built our house tucked under a hill
         up above the mushroom woods

He came home walking back from the train after the war
He loved me once each night
Again in the morning so we wouldn't forget

Sometimes we walked all day
We saw so many pretty places
Sometimes I left my eyes there

And now?

You
         now that you're older
You have all the beauty of your mother
         with none of your grandfather's stink!

Keep your house—keep it
         tight as a ship and twice as neat

[She pours and they drink.]

Mother Comes

Was I a boy or a girl?

Both and neither. It took me a while to figure that out.

Thirty, forty years?

Long enough to know I didn't know. You burned the candle at both ends.

I've had great love affairs.

And suffered the consequences. Kto wie, daughter.

What was it with the big blue book?

Oh, everybody had that in the fifties. Your father & I got one. Even the priest knew.

Lots of pillows, positioning of the woman for the convenience of the man!

Haven't you learned anything by now?

Ha. You only taught me your idols:
Thoreau a virgin: Leopardi a virgin:
Dickinson maybe   probably not   maybe   No
wonder I was confused.

Babies are babies, the two who died I still think of.

How did you grieve?

We drove to Erie and threw our sorrows in.
We drove to Niagara and threw more in.
We drove to Chicago to the Shrine of Saint Jude. You were conceived.

Why Are You Wearing Your Father's Sweater?

The patterns are telling me something.
And I'm still grieving.

You have it bad, the chiemny melancholia. You have too much time on your hands.

I haven't even started grieving you yet.

Death is a mistake. I had to quit for the day. That was it.

Who was Satin Head you were calling when we got to the ER?

That young Afro-American nurse. He helped me turn on my side, then pulled me
                                                          through.
Yanked is more like it.

I thought I heard you two singing.

No, I told him my poem, the one about the "old women in the death throes . . . tears
carving hot ditches down their cheeks . . . "

You were 90: weren't you a little bit ready?

You think I'm old? You took me out of my house, you took all my dresses.

Is that why you staged the break-in in your room the week you moved into the
                                                          place?

Of course I did. You kids have no idea

" . . . what it's like to go into a place." Ma, we've learned a little. It's here for us soon too.

All I need is my Level Green yard & my Matka Ziema

[Mother prays:]

The willow grows & gives:
Her baskets hold the laundry,
so line them with good linen.
For your summer party under the willow tree
line them with old linen, & towels,
then ice, then 50 green bottles of beer!
And when your neighbor dies
line them with good linen
place warm bread, butter, salty ham
and carry them next door.

I grieve the gardens too. They're overgrown.

Did you take the lily bulbs, a myrtle cutting, the heart of my hearts: rock geranium?

All.

Did You Place Wishes in the Four Walls?

Did you?

All.
And I learned to read under the forsythia.

That's all you did. Read until you burnt your eyes. Give me the eye cup.

She Pours Boric Acid & Water into the Eye Cup

Better. You don't realize
it doesn't stop—
to want to—
and not be able to see.

Tell me about the veils.

They began two years before Satin Head pulled me out. My mother, my brothers
Walter the violinist & Stacey the collector of rocks & coins. Your father was there the
whole time of the in-between. He was teaching me when I was still able to walk. I call
this "Two Veils" for him:

> I feel it lifting itself & floating
> behind me on the path, cooling
> the small of my back.
>
> A partition or wall made of leaves
> & air that follows me past the long
> hedges of pink roses
>
> along the parking lot of the place.
> Darling, when you had less than a day
> staring at your hospital curtain
>
> you studied its plastic rungs & bright
> chevrons & boomerangs for your tossing,
> and sat up & grabbed that sail.
>
> "I'm working," you said, reading
> your curtain while you shook off
> your strokes, & choking in that room
>
> of green walls & foul sheets
> you entered something new.

His tent, the shelter he was building for the two of you.

There is no shelter. But there's work, plenty of it.

Is that why you started painting again?

*Oh, those classes were a joke. Formulas & stencils. I am a colorist following shapes.
Refill my cup.*

Chamomile, goldenseal, an icy spoon: better.

Boric acid, acid rain, fracking juice. [Laughs.]

Did we break each other's hearts when you left?

A little, maybe. But greater troubles: the wars, the cancers, for starters.

The wars, the clock ticking on our Sun.

*It's still got 5 or so billion years, our Sun . . .
the slaughters . . . the hungers . . .*

The hearts, our hearts, our burst hearts.

III.

Smoky summer evening from the high sky-
light swirls sun-flares inside the shadows
and singes my heart with its seal.

—Dino Campana

Crystal Bar

*—purest form of zirconium fabricated for use in dentistry,
    orthopedics, and nuclear reactors*

*—. . . the Sun rays, when periodically intercepted, would cause blows of
    such force on my brain that they would stun me*

—Nicola Tesla

Brown pools
flood my father's brittle Polaroids,
I try to read them like coffee dregs,
fuel rods swollen
in water inside the reactor.
Beside them I lay the crisp black & white
company-issue glossy

of his calibration tool.
I call it his harp,
small enough to slide
into a pocket.
Bent over his graph paper with square
lead pencil he drew the harp freehand,
metal butter his chosen medium, *crystal bar*

so he could tune-
in for others
what he heard and remembered—

the Seabees radio frequency, Manos Island
hours before sirens screamed VJ Day,
or later, underwater, listening in the fifties
on the Nautilus, vibrations in the visor
of his welding helmet.

Your harp
never bore your patent, only the letter
W, robbed for Westinghouse's starry fortune.

Phonons buzzed against the walls
of your inner ear,
along your soul-strings;
phone chips, watch casings,
pacemakers   tools we hold to hear you now.

I'm looking for you in the rhomboid mirrors
of the metal-butter chunk
you brought home.

Sentences from My Father, 1967–1970

*—from letters; Repair & Refuel assignment,
Fermi Reactor, Piedmont*

Dear Angel and Kids—

The plant is located 50 miles above Torino in a town located not above the
mountains or below them but between the clouds.

Today ENEL from Rome hired four divers to take some measurements for me but the radiation
rate was too high for them to enter the pool and I was thrilled to build an additional tool to
eliminate their task, remotely.

This is not a big country it is just a long one. What surprises me more is why they gave us a tough
go in the war? It would be like Pitcairn fighting the US now in my opinion. No kidding, it is just
like the Westinghouse Valley with St. Coleman's being the head of it all.

It is so foggy that you can't see 20 feet before you and I am told it is this way 6 months out of the
year. Fiat Company is located here and these people are going wild spending money.

Last night I heard a violinist play like I never heard before and I met a priest who teaches in Cali-
fornia. He picked me up this morning and took me to St. Peter's where he said mass. After mass
we had lunch of salami and "birra."

I drove through Rome and it is all anyone can say about it good and bad. If you drive to an open
spot everyone wants it so if you close your eyes and gas it you have it made!

They showed a movie on the plane coming over but I didn't watch it because they had a real fine
stereo at all seats with 9 channels and I listened all night. My task here is much easier than at
Yankee because the plant is much larger and the equipment is wonderful.

The mountains here in Vercelli stick right through the clouds—the pilot had to make three
approaches before getting in through the fog and my nose started to bleed.

The only difference between these people and at home is that here there are definitely two classes. One class is old ladies riding bikes with wood in bundles to town for sale or cleaning streets and the other class is in riding habits walking through the shops.

The fog is so bad that even the president of Russia is coming in by train. I am sure to see him tomorrow because he is having lunch at this hotel and is to visit Fiat where I too am going to be located. Mr. DiAnna took me to dinner this evening to talk over common problems and to teach me the safe way an Italian drinks wine!

I do believe that if I demand a real value for this caper I can get it because who else could do this to make circle-W uncle George Westinghouse ¼ million dollars?

On Saturday Herb, Nick, John, Bill, Vince and I went to the Italian Mediterranean town of Genova. The water is truly blue and the ships are a real sight. No swimming because of the dirty contaminated water—

We worked overtime all last week and I think we are finally at the base of our troubles! The Italians must have driven this reactor like they do a Fiat and as a result ruined it. I was glad to hear Bob is now captain and Jude is home to clean the basement early HAHA I do miss Jude getting my ice cream!

My contact man is to go to war in Israel on Monday because he was on ready call.

We are moving fuel and evaluating damage which will take us another two weeks and I will be free for a long time. I didn't know a man my age could get homesick but I guess I will never grow up. The food tastes better now that I got used to the benzene taste of oil.

Every afternoon we walk along the Po River which is almost like Oil City but I never saw so many fish in one spot. The trout are the biggest ever and the fishermen keep pulling them in with traps that look like boxes with screens on three sides.

I sure wish I had my old gray jacket! I hate to ruin my topcoat everywhere I go even to the junk heap they call a reactor.

I think Italy is held together by the women. They do all the work and the men didn't lift a hand for 50 years.

▲ ▲ ▲

Today we found real troubles in the reactor! So it is only a matter of time until we will be asked to leave.

▲ ▲ ▲

Water is more expensive than beer and scotch and it's surely a mixed up country. And our group got paid to inspect this reactor. A child could see they were not doing a good job. Engineers at Westinghouse are not even good laborers and I intend to tell them about it.

▲ ▲ ▲

I had to buy a transistor radio because my room doesn't have music or news. I just came back from church and everyone likes my coat. We are now about to write up our investigation of plant damage and I informed the manager that I have had it.

▲ ▲ ▲

The weather is frosty but clear and we intend to go for a walk this afternoon. Yesterday Nick and I went to Milan and the stores are all ready for Christmas. I looked for bags for 4 hours but found none that you would like I am sure.

▲ ▲ ▲

Last night Herb had his car stolen and the police insisted he go to Milan to tell why he thought a locked car could be taken from up here in the Alps. They were even looking behind trees too small to hide a car and teasing him that way and even though Herb lost his camera it was worth it.

▲ ▲ ▲

Mr. Stratta is preparing pheasant for us tonight because I refused to eat his blackbirds. He leaves the heads on so the juice won't run out and man what a dish! Funghi omelets are my dish! Many of the young people here have been asking me what they have to earn to live in the US because they all want to go.

▲ ▲ ▲

Our work is not going fast enough. I had 5 minutes more to go on an underwater measurement after it took me 2 days to set up for it and an operator turned off the TV because it was lunch time. Tomorrow I have to start over again.

▲ ▲ ▲

Rome this time looks just like the North Side of Pittsburgh before they tore it down. Then again I think this hotel is really out of this world. I am told the Pope is sick but I intend to go there again anyway.

▲ ▲ ▲

I intend to hand-carry the Italian newspapers for you because mailing them is over $25. All of the stores carry everything for Christmas and although everyone is passing through the stores no one is taking any packages home, they only look.

▲ ▲ ▲

The flight goes first to Geneva then to NY and Pgh so you see we can go shopping in Pgh on the 23rd. The weather is so bright that I had to buy another pair of sunglasses. If the fog stays away you can see mountains 60 miles away. I think Bob and Jude are wonderful and I keep praying Rege soon gets his word one way or another. I am listening to "My Baby and Me" in German believe it or not. All month the fellas have been spending evenings playing cards in my room because I have the music.

▲ ▲ ▲

Dave Edgar and wife arrived and she seems very nice. He will work in Turin following our hardware while it is being manufactured over Christmas. Enough shop talk for tonight because I must say I love you all and I do miss you very much. I can't read the papers here and there are no Italian cowboys so I might as well say my prayers and go to bed.

Love   Be careful
Dad

Dear Sky Travelers

—Pittsburgh's hillside pedestrian stairways cover 23+ city miles;
80 percent are concrete, the rest are wood, brick, steel, asphalt

Up the first 50 snowy steps to the bluff
I catch the sun's flaming pink sliver.
Someone sprinkled kosher salt, good
for baking bread & melting snow to lace.
50 more tongues clack, I look down
on a skeleton-arbor & bag of old shoes'
rotten threads, past Pig Alley
to the slaughterhouse blood that fed the multiflora
rimming the workroom where Aunt
read the paper to men who rolled cigars.
Patched wood, dented waffle-steel. Wind-burned.
Some must know them all by heart.
I'm stumbling inside folds she moved into

& out of—she forgets a word, so I
write it, leave it for the priest floating
above a stilt-house one cliff over,
he loves her Monday baking.
Across the ball-field in Spring Garden
the pharmacy steams from last night's fire. Note on door:

INFO WILL BE POSTED HERE.
NO RECORDS LOST.

All around the perimeter
in silver rain a thousand street lamps
click off. Up past the shed Aunt stocked with cans
of beans & jugs of water for strangers,
I walk above
twenty-six centuries worth of shelter.
Across the river the all-night men shovel hot asphalt,
work flags snapping, metal tools scraping.
The road snakes, no berms or
guardrails yet, only the line unrolling

against earth-slabs, storm ruts, & the backlit
cement-block tracts. Locked warehouses of
sheetrock & giant bracelet-link ironworks
sleep until the governor stretches a finger
in our direction.
                    Down Speck Street's steps a last
retaining wall props the ghost-garage

VOLLMER TRANSFER

*WE'LL MOVE YOU TO WHEELING, BUFFALO,
ALL THE WAY TO NEW YORK CITY*

the 1-truck hauling business where Pap
sang into the phone on the wall:
*We're back from a job up Montreal Monday,
Tuesday you're in your own home!*

Cherrypicker driver lifts another
steel pipe, swings it precisely to
his buddy who unfastens it, lays it down
through the drizzle lit with bright headlamps.
                              I stop
for a pony bottle of Coke & a protein
bar at the artifact Sunoco,
washroom tacked to its side, travelers'
haven, 4th generation, swabbed down,
fresh zinnias in July, plastic holly all winter.
                    Aunt was a dervish
scrubbing steps: commandant of April:
teeth out, skirt pinned up:
*Yu-ditt-a, I carry the bucket   you take the steel brush
& we wash'm all down*
                         I trip over the roots
of Mount Troy summit's skinny pine,
sit, sweaty, happy in my all-day January thaw.
12 miles, 11 or so to go,
around, up and down
the 9 hills.

Bookending the downtown the two ghost-hotels:
The Fort Pitt where the Gunia Girls sang
with flowers in their hair during the War
& the Monongahela House: Twain, Lincoln
slept there above The Wharf.
They could glimpse the river
through the infernos.

Dear sky travelers:
in your 2-second heart-beat fly-
over, see our ground-level wonder
which, stair-by-stairway,
lifted into the air all at once
reaches exactly the Everest Summit.

IV.

Let me stay here inside so much
wing and leaf motion, and hear the rooster
calling from one farm, and from another
the other answers.

—Giovanni Pascoli

Little Death

She will rip some hair from your head

Pluck pearls from your spine

She will open you

She will knock your teeth out

She scrapes at your sweetmeats

Her own vulva gone rancid

And last she will drain your tender

Eye sockets   prancing with your eyes in her palm

With them she'll look around the universe

Seeing endless rings & spirals

For the first time

     Your tendons   your bones

     Sticks on the ground still working

     Themselves in their mother language

Last Effects, Old House

Two flint points   1 for cutting grain   1 for meat

This paring knife for cleaning Grandfather's teeth

Bowie I keep in my high shoes

Red serrated I've never used
        against myself or anyone else

If you're thinking omissions are lies

I could care less

My saw-toothed story I'll keep
        using to slice

tomatoes & warm rosemary bread

Mother Wall

Through the wall that might lead
to the thimble paths
or the petunia bed

or through the indigo window-
wall facing west

I reach for her

but every time I put my fist through

my arm comes back
clung with auburn hair gone to ash
or bottles of clotted rouge.

Street Grate

Pocked sentry—
so many years you've looked up into the long seasons'
white-hot suns
& black-ice roofs.
Scarred bronze eye—
I wonder how many times you've seen

the fledgling screech owls'
silhouettes nightly between 10:30 & 11
on the sycamore branch above you?

8 bars across   12 down
ALLEGHENY CITY DEPARTMENT OF PUBLIC WORKS 1936
[8 pitted bronze horizontal bars/12 pitted verticals]

Smashed glass & matted rot-mouth;
rat cage-top my uncles
breathed through in the hell tunnels
they had to scrape by hand,

I hope you know the cat,
leather pads stepping
carefully   bar to bar
big fur belly hanging down
brushing you,
hole for rushing waters,
dear steel eye span.

58

The Shape-up

—temporary hiring site

Steps above the expressway
they want the young student
      w/ good command of basic English
to clean the loft or snip strings from jackets.
She, on the overpass, suffers changing weather,
folds unfolds her legs
on off a bus every day
      stands on hot asphalt to be or not selected
by strangers who offer
day-pay. Noon she vanishes
after swift negotiations, 20 cents below Minimum. Space
she took on the Brooklyn-Queens Expressway
is a sliver pattern
I'm living in my mind, can't-get-out pattern, mothers
fight for 20 cents below Minimum.
I'm here to give a poetry reading,
I told her this, woman I met
while waiting for a bus in mammoth
September's 88-degree morning.
We were trying to talk to each other,
Polish, English, reverse, start over.
One time she ended up in the wrong
building, elevator with a stuck
emergency button & a day-boss
twice her size. I asked but knew better.

After Reading Another Book of Dull Poetry,
I Go Out and Cut the Grass

Thrash blades furiously, obliterate
all, stain flagstones green

stagger to hose for cold drink, steaming
& also smeared green, 8 minutes, done.
The fragrance I love? Volatiles spewing

their delicious distress call
so now I feel sad about my violence

once pouring leftover paint down the cellar
sink, burning plastic, etc. Big prize
book in today's mail so smart so icy

I ripped the cover off & tossed guts.
Usually it is very hard to write a poem

sometimes as much   sometimes far less
than Rachel Carson's labor finishing
Silent Spring, she who let her grass grow

freely up in Springdale
even when neighbors complained, she who
concurred with William Douglas
roadside flowers also have inalienable rights,

who labored to simplify her book
while suffering last chemo   so the public
could read & comprehend it.
Smart poets:

Thurgood Marshall, after a hard day
on the bench loved to repair to chambers,
turn on, unwind to *The People's Court*.
My Subaru-sized yard is not a handkerchief of the lord

90% turned over for vegetables & flowers,
but I take a sec   admire cut velvet heightening
the lilies, and the birdbath visible 360°.

Flower Meal

I slid the sliver of anchovy that holds the sea
inside the cube of robiola, and that
I slid inside the flower.

When I pinched the blossom shut
I kissed it
dipped it in egg, flour & the golden oil

then carried it on the white plate
and when you lifted it to your mouth
did you remember?

Every flower is a savant—
Only last night your mother
was waiting for you here on Via Merulana

and remember, you'd just read
the strange novel with that title
and then a word from a stranger

brought you to my table
where the jasmine loves to fall onto the dark
zucchini, so when I

with my hands   open & fill
this orange flower
have I not opened you too?

A hungry mouth,
which is voice—
& your salt-sweet restless soul?

My Mother's Paintings

Now I understand the theory of relativity
she tells her 8 companions,
8 shaking brushes above pre-drawn Easter baskets
& elephants—long life!—above plastic
bowls of mauves & greens.
Near-blind my mother dips
into the paints' slow gusto
and daphnes a line into a slender tree.
I prefer abstractions, she snaps,
indicating her basket's handle with pointillistic jerks
of her good wrist. Her elephant
tosses its trunk off the paper onto the table
& floor the aide will mop.
Freehand she stitched portraits on our
jean jackets: Hendrix guitar for Bob,
sleeping-girl-under-willow for me.
Her finished piece
hangs on the lobby wall at the far
end of the row—she's up front
leading the parade! I beam
rushing in after work
toward her golden basket
& wandering elephant
to see how she's signed:

her initial: *T*
& scratched along the bottom:
Yesterday Lonely   Today Running Free

Copper, Gold, Olives, Wine

—to Apollonia

No one way to be a woman
No one way to be a city
But I know your many cities, whether
Greek, Czech, Polish, or Slovenian,
I know your copper bracelets,
your rivers of destruction.

No way to save yourself & no one
to save you, 249 A.D. Alexandria;
Bernardino's later portrait: in your right hand
a book & colossal pincers
to vanquish torturers;
in your left, the martyr's palm frond.

Woman of no one place, Portuguese,
Brazilian, woman of Suzussa—famous
crayfish & wine! Of Sozopol,
Pontica, and Pollina Sicilia,
so many places bear your name;
you are honored here too:
bowl of olives & oil, glass with a worn
gold rim, in this house built on Pennsylvania
soil, old earth, many times over
burred & extracted.

In Praise of Margaret Drabble

*—excerpts & fragments from an interview with
Margaret Drabble, London, 1997*

"Be completely cut off. Finish one thing begin another. If you know where you're going the material is in that filing system. Which isn't always true. You can get stuck: did you throw it away, did you shove off with it altogether?

When I was writing about Cambodia & Vietnam how to confront the reader with places they didn't know or care to back then? I went back over & back over that book not wanting it to be smoothly joined, wanted it to have this violent contrast, jerking myself mood to mood, scene or setting—like a patchwork—get the rhythm right & keep waking up in a panic.

That character was a man of great charm when he was around. You could say you felt he was always looking for, he was always on a search, & I was intrigued (& I was never quite clear what Joseph Conrad's own moral position on Imperialism was)—something very distasteful there—I was intrigued by this character this man who seemed not to fit.

I wonder if Conrad had been alive now, of what he would have made of the collapse of the Socialist dream or of the very real structured & delightful aspects of capitalism or the chaos of the relative response now & lack of moral certainty & the withdrawal toward poverty & suffering.

Coincidence & fate are a question of taking your chances & not refusing them. This takes a great deal of courage in life. In not being frightened & not saying no. Or moving in & out of things. My second marriage has lasted longer than my first; it seems like it was yesterday I got married again.

I wake up, get up at seven, sort of have a cup of coffee & then just start to work straightaway and back at it. Really kind of like a child. Sort out the work, & that usually lasts me till lunchtime & then a rest & then an evening walk.

▲ ▲ ▲

So when I was finishing that book I set off around four or five in the afternoon & walked for a couple of hours thinking about the next day's work & that was the most creative time for me because I was walking & not sitting & staring at a typewriter. There were other good impulses coming in from nature & the sound & the veil—whatever you could feel. Whatever you could feel. I'll give you one concrete example of that.

One evening when I was in absolute despair about the end of the novel & what to do with him & the _____ & the _____ & how to wrap all that lot up. I mean I didn't know what to do with them.

▲ ▲ ▲

I didn't know where that group of people were during that point of history. I really know much better now than I did when I was writing. I mean I know where they are now.

▲ ▲ ▲

They were then, absolutely & utterly mysteriously where they were & what they were. And I drove my car, it was six o'clock, the six o'clock news, it must have been a summer evening, a beautiful summer evening, & I thought, so I'll just listen to the news. And there was an item on ____ & how there was said to be an encampment in _____ & lighting campfires, & for what, a ceremony.

And I thought, my god, they've claimed to have taken that land from the Vietnamese & I went for my walk in this utterly English beautiful woodland thinking about civilians caught in war & suddenly that last bit kind of fell into a thought pattern.

▲ ▲ ▲

And the very end scenes, of him & the amazing storm, of the hail stones & the girls dancing—that just came to me, because I was sitting writing in my car about the dance which I'd just seen. And the most amazing storm broke out over London & I thought I'd never seen anything like it. I thought: that's what happens, some kind of natural manifestation. And so there's a wonderful way in which nature itself (I know it doesn't sound very worthy) I mean nature itself will come and help you.

⚠ ⚠ ⚠

Coincidence, like switching on, I mean I must have known this, in some bits of my brain. Or I may have read something. Who knows. I was not particularly utterly unaware of it, but there are people all around us nevertheless leading fairly responsible, free, and liberated lives.

⚠ ⚠ ⚠

Then I think of the geological layers of co-existing freedom and bondage and dependence & all the rest of it going on. I think I'm reporting what is, rather than what people say ought to be.

⚠ ⚠ ⚠

Odd, sometimes you hear things you can't use because you're writing the wrong kind of book. So you hope you can remember them if you ever need them later. And sometimes they drop straight into what you're working on. If something has a sort of glimmer, an invitation in it, one should on the whole say yes."

The Looting of Cerveteri

Long before the Euphronios cup, rarest red & black
      —Etrusca gold—vase for wine or tears—
was repatriated from the Getty & set

      in Villa Giulia's glass case "lit with tiny bulbs
                like Christmas lights"

an exhausted man   face masked with dirt
      blinked & trembled at white sun
          rode his rail cart up out of earth-mouth,
stash unsorted till he got home.

His girl plucked out
      a libation bowl rimmed with golden acorns
         while the man wedged broken pilasters
      into his south wall against winds.

See the carts bumping along tracks
      out of the necropoli of Chaco,
         Tripoli, Palmyra—

Perhaps the dying
      store their house & temple
treasures for a future just like the girl's
who gathers owl feathers
dresses the cup with them as she would a doll

small fingers resting in the bowl
      happy with her feathers.

notes

The word *druzhba* on the dedication page is "beloved friend" in Ukrainian.

The Pavese epigraph opening section I is from his verse/prose *Dialogues with Leucò*, translated by William Arrowsmith (Eridanos Press, 1989). The epigraphs opening sections II and III are excerpted from my translations of Giuseppe Ungaretti's "I Have Lost Everything" and Dino Campana's "Skylight," which were published in *Mead: The Magazine of Literature and Libations*. The epigraph opening section IV, excerpted from Giovanni Pascoli's "Time at Barga," is also my translation.

"Window with Bottles" is for Michael Waters; for our mothers. Lines 12–20 are a variation and compression of three sentences found in Book V of Lucretius' *On the Nature of the Universe*, translated by R. E. Latham (Penguin Books, 1951).

"Walking to *Miami*" is for Erjola Tafaj.

"Children of October" is for Max Begler and Anne Marie Macari. The poem was inspired, in part, by a phrase from Carlo Emilio Gadda's novel *That Awful Mess on the Via Merulana*, translated by William Weaver (New York Review Books, 2006).

Italicized phrases in "White Box   Blue Lid" are from the title poem of William Stafford's *Allegiances* (Harper & Row, 1970). The JAMBLOCK is a patented security device invented by Pennsylvania high school teacher Bob Ploskunak.

"The Transfer" was inspired by the work of American Abstract Expressionist Joan Mitchell (1925–1992).

"The Vowel" is for Marisa Frasca.

"The Apollonia Sequence":

> *Mala Babka*: Little Grandmother;
>
> *Jaskółka: The Swallow*, twentieth-century weekly newspaper published in Rzeszow, Poland;
>
> *Sticker Hollow*: local Pittsburgh name for hawthorn-wooded riverbank that became a company housing neighborhood adjacent to Henry Clay Frick's Coraopolis coal mine along the Youghiogheny River;
>
> *Matki Bozej Czestokowa*: Black Madonna of Czestochowa;
>
> *Wisniak*: cherry brandy, or vodka, depending on recipe;
>
> *You / now that you're older / You have all the beauty of your mother / with none of your grandfather's stink!*: variation on a sentence from *The Leopard* by Giuseppe di Lampedusa, translated by Archibald Colquhoun (Pantheon, 1960);
>
> *Kto wie?*: Who knows?;
>
> *chiemny melancholia*: dark melancholy or moodiness;
>
> *Matka Ziema*: moist earth, or "Damp Mother Earth," oldest deity in Slavic mythology; similar to Indo-Iranian Ardvi Sura Anahita "Humid Mother of the Earth"; frequently honored at graveside with a jar of hemp oil, or lavender, or coins, which are then buried with the dead.

"The Shape-up" is after *New York Times* reporter Nina Bernstein.

WISCONSIN POETRY SERIES
Ronald Wallace, *Series Editor*

(B) = Winner of the Brittingham Prize in Poetry
(FP) = Winner of the Felix Pollak Prize in Poetry
(4L) = Winner of the Four Lakes Prize in Poetry

Ripe (FP) • Roy Jacobstein

Saving the Young Men of Vienna (B) • David Kirby

Falling Brick Kills Local Man (FP) • Mark Kraushaar

Last Seen (FP) • Jacqueline Jones LaMon

The Lightning That Strikes the Neighbors' House (FP) • Nick Lantz

You, Beast (B) • Nick Lantz

The Unbeliever (B) • Lisa Lewis

Slow Joy (B) • Stephanie Marlis

Acts of Contortion (B) • Anna George Meek

Bardo (B) • Suzanne Paola

Meditations on Rising and Falling (B) • Philip Pardi

Old and New Testaments (B) • Lynn Powell

A Path between Houses (B) • Greg Rappleye

The Book of Hulga (FP) • Rita Mae Reese

Don't Explain (FP) • Betsy Sholl

Late Psalm • Betsy Sholl

Otherwise Unseeable (4L) • Betsy Sholl

Blood Work (FP) • Matthew Siegel

The Year We Studied Women (FP) • Bruce Snider

Bird Skin Coat (B) • Angela Sorby

The Sleeve Waves (FP) • Angela Sorby

Wait (B) • Alison Stine

Hive (B) • Christina Stoddard

The Red Virgin: A Poem of Simone Weil (B) • Stephanie Strickland

The Room Where I Was Born (B) • Brian Teare

Fragments in Us: Recent and Earlier Poems (FP) • Dennis Trudell

The Apollonia Poems (4L) • Judith Vollmer

Level Green (B) • Judith Vollmer

Reactor • Judith Vollmer

Voodoo Inverso (FP) • Mark Wagenaar

Hot Popsicles • Charles Harper Webb

Liver (FP) • Charles Harper Webb

The Blue Hour (B) • Jennifer Whitaker

Centaur (B) • Greg Wrenn

Pocket Sundial (B) • Lisa Zeidner